Happy Thirteenth Birthday

13 REASONS WHY YOU'RE AMAZING

"The most effective
way to do it,
is to do it."

-AMELIA EARHEART

Reason #1

"You are enough.
Just the way you are.
Just who you are."

-ANONYMOUS

Reason #2

"It is better to conquer yourself than to win a thousand battles.
Then the victory is yours."

-BUDDHA

Reason #3

"I have not failed.
I've just found 10,000
ways that don't work."

-THOMAS EDISON

Reason #4

"The other girls?
They've got nothing on you."

-ANONYMOUS

Reason #5

"The best way to predict the future is to create it."

-ABRAHAM LINCOLN

Reason #6

"Beauty is created by your attitude, your behaviour & your actions."

-ANONYMOUS

Reason #7

"Happiness and confidence are the prettiest things you can wear."

-TAYLOR SWIFT

Reason #8

"Always be a first
rate version of yourself,
instead of a second rate
version of someone else."

-JUDY GARLAND

Reason #9

"Courage doesn't always roar. Sometimes courage is the quiet voice at the end of the day saying, "I will try again tomorrow."

-MARY A RADMACHER

Reason #10

"The difference between winning and losing is most often not quitting."

-WALT DISNEY

Reason #11

"No one can make you feel inferior without your consent."

-ELEANOR ROOSEVELT

Reason #12

"Always chase your dreams instead of running from your fears."

-ANONYMOUS

Reason #13

Did you enjoy this book?

If so, help others enjoy it too.

Please recommend to friends and leave a review when possible!

Thanks,

THERE ARE HEAPS MORE AMAZING CARDS

Girls & Boys Happy Birthday
Reasons You Are Amazing
Ages 8 - 21

Happy Birthday for Women
What Makes You Amazing
60, 65, 70, 75, 85-100

Mens Happy Birthday
Reasons Why You Are Amazing
50, 55, 60, 65, 70, 75, 80,
85, 90, 95, 100

Women Happy Birthday
Reasons Why You Are Amazing
30th, 40th, 50th, 60th

Bogus
BIRTHDAY CARDS

FIND US ON AMAZON

Made in the USA
Coppell, TX
09 November 2022

86080728R00018